Topic Based
Concepts

MANGESH DAMBHARE

ISBN: 9798687585989

Price: $9 (USD)

Disclaimer

Book Cover Design: Mangesh Dambhare

DEDICATION

Hare Kṛṣṇa Hare Kṛṣṇa

Kṛṣṇa Kṛṣṇa Hare Hare
Hare Rāma Hare Rāma
Rāma Rāma Hare Hare

CONTENTS

3. The Way of Life

4. Analysis

5. Curiosity

6. Art & Design

TOPIC BASED CONCEPTS

PREFACE

This book provides you with concepts based on different topics of general studies. It will add up some knowledge about various topics of global interests and a wide spectrum of thoughts and ideas.

World View, Top Rated, The Way of Life, Analysis, Curiosity, Art & Design are key modules covered in this copy of the book. This book generates in you a clear view of the topics in order to keep you organized.

1. World View

TOPIC BASED CONCEPTS

1.1 GEOPOLITICS ON THE PLANET EARTH

Change in Perspective

We already knew that the perspective of warfare in geopolitics has been completely changed over the course of time. That's why the identification of real friends and enemies has become a major concern for all the countries in the world. Broadly there are few formations of groups of countries as power players in world politics, recently we can notice.

Alliances of Powers

The Western alliance is powerful along with the emerging multi-polar world. There are now five major groups seem to be growing superpower entity. Those can be identified as follows:

(a) Western Alliance - The United States of America, Major European Countries, Australia, Japan, and some of the countries in the middle east and Asia-pacific.

(b) Eastern Power Block – China, Iran along with some countries in Middle East.

Independent Claims – (c) India & (d) Russia

(e) Flow-Aligned Countries – Countries playing role reserving interest depending on the changing conditions.

Growing Nationalism

The idea of becoming self-sufficient is taking an important place in the vision and development plans of almost every country. The Role of geopolitics will be based on this idea to become more strengthened and self-sufficient. Growing nationalism will not allow conquering the borders of the nations and the status quo will be always mostly maintained for a long period of time. It has been more rigid than ever and would be.

Next World War

There will no world war take place among the countries on the planet due to the theory of deterrence. They will definitely unite one day in the future due to the next war against enemies from outer space. At that time soul of the world will be purified by winning over against the inner evil spirit.

Era of Transformations

In every aspect of living beings on this planet, a huge transformation can be and will be seen. Transformations of mind and power on the planet are taking place and we must wake up to become an active part of it.

1.2 THE MAJOR DEFENCE POWERS AN OVERVIEW

United States, India, Russia, China and The European Union are the major defence powers seems to be emerging global superpowers in the new multi-polar world order.

United States

<u>Capabilities</u>

The Defence budget of The United States of America is the highest spending on military expenditure in the world and may reach the mark of annually one trillion US dollar in the next decade. Equipped with advanced hi-tech technological arms the military capability of the USA is unmatched in the world. Fifth generation stealth fighter aircrafts like F-22 and F-35 fighters, nuclear-powered submarines and the largest fleet carriers in the world, Extended Range Interceptor, Space Surveillance and Tracking System and Innovative Directed Energy Weapon Programs, these are the super strengths of the US Military.

Accompanied by the innovations by The National Aeronautics and Space Administration (NASA) and multiethnic brainpower, the US is the most advanced defence power in the world.

<u>Alliance</u>

The United States of America and the NATO (North Atlantic Treaty Organization) alliance of western power can prove the toughest defence shield in the world.

India

<u>Capabilities</u>

Armed with zealous patriotism and the toughest combating skills with large multitalented active troops, Indian defence forces are ready to conquer any challenges to the world peace. India is emerging as a global power player in the defence sector with world-class armed preparations and strategic planning. India has the capability to lead the world in outlining strategic defence plans and policies. It has the strong capability to deter the aggressions against the humanities.

Latest military reforms, enough military spending, major arms importer and exporter, and building strategic defence partnerships with the nations on the ground of common interest are key strengths of India's Military Capabilities. India is a powerful command in strategically important Indian Ocean Region.

India has indomitable armed forces with Special Frontier Force, Marine & Garud Commandos, and Ghatak Force. As a defence power equipped with advanced fighter aircrafts like Rafale, Sukhoi 30 Mirage 2000, and HAL Tejas, Nuclear-Capable Indian Ballistic Missile Defence Programme, and World-Class Submarines, India can deter any military might on this planet.

<u>Alliance</u>

India has maintained good and strategic relations with all major counties and power blocks in the world. India is an active participant of The Quadrilateral Security Dialogue Forum between the United States, Japan, Australia and India. India has also maintained good relations with Russia, Israel, France, Vietnam and some Gulf countries. India held many joint military exercises with the United States, Japan, Russia, France, Kazakhstan, Mongolia and also was two times participant in Exercise Red Flag by the United States Air Force.

Russia

<u>Capabilities</u>

Russia has decades of spending on innovations and technology since the soviet era. Hi-tech and severely powerful military technologies are Russia's unique strength and capacity builders. Armed with Fifth-generation jet fighters like Sukhoi Su-57, S-500 missile system, world-class nuclear submarines, advancements in space technology are the great strengths of the military of the Russian Federation.

Alliance

Russia has maintained its diplomatic relations with all major countries in the world. Russia has bilateral relations with many countries in almost all continents and this is Russia's special capability to deal with any type of situation in the world scenario.

China

Capabilities

With the military strength equipped with Fifth-generation jet fighter like J-20, nuclear submarines and high defence spending China is trying to cope up with the challenges emerged due do to its policies.

Alliance

China has strategic and diplomatic relations with many countries in the world. China also has built good relations with most of the countries.

European Union

Capabilities

Countries in the European Union are individually of great strengths indeed and they have come together to form a strong military alliance power in the world. Innovative defence technologies and arms, the European Union plays an important role in military build-ups in the world.

Manufacturer of advanced fighter planes like the Eurofighter Typhoon, building up strong defence shields, and advance maritime and space ventures are notable strengths of the European Union.

Alliance

The European Union is a constituent of the alliance of mostly all developed European countries. The formation of the NATO alliance for creating and maintaining peace among the region and continents was very essential. European Union and NATO forces have a great influence on the EMEA region.

TOPIC BASED CONCEPTS

1.3 TOP ECONOMIES AND MARKETS

In a few words let's try to take an overview of top economies and markets in the world. Business markets around the world are operated through investments and financial operations.

Top Economies

Rise of India

US, China, India, Japan and the European Union are the top economies which influence businesses all over the world. India will surpass China until 2035 if the growth of India's Economy will soar high. Financial reforms by the government of India 2014 onwards and entrepreneurs' rising aspirations in India are creating potential and grounds for the sustainable growth in the upcoming future. Business-friendly policies and the new educational policy will act as reviving agents in boosting the economy.

Group of Nations

Overview

Big Four, G7, G10, G20, EU, NATO, BRICS, ASEAN, BIMSTEC, OPEC etc. are the groups of countries driving the economic activities around the world. The World is so connected with each other through the exchange of ideas, that the leading force is distributed among the nations on this planet.

Stock Exchanges in the World

<u>Over view</u>

Stock markets function through major stock exchanges in the world and some of them are The New York Stock Exchange (NYSE), Nasdaq, Shanghai Stock Exchange (SSE), Bombay Stock Exchange (BSE), Euronext, London Stock Exchange (LSE), Japan Exchange Group (JPX), etc.

1.4 INDIA IS BECOMING VISHWA GURU

New Sustainable Path

India started its new sustainable path of development in all aspects. India is progressing on this path on all fronts.

Political Will

The great political will of our leader of the nation taking the nation to achieve a new high. In the leadership of Honorable Prime Minister Narendra Modi, India is constantly making good progress towards becoming a Global Superpower. He is so focused on the planned framework of achievements.

People's Contribution

The most important major contribution of the people of India in the progress of the nation is that they have shown strong confidence in the leadership of Shri. Narendra Modi and elected him for the next consecutive term. This enabled him to continue with the policies for achieving the milestones which were set on the agenda considering the long term effects on the transformation of the nation into a powerful country in the world, so that every Indian will feel proud and will be honored with great importance on the global platform.

Powerful Reforms

Major powerful reforms that have been introduced and will be proposed by the Modi government should be studied carefully and understood taking note of its importance. Those can be a guideline for policymakers all over the world.

Major Reforms

Business-friendly economic reforms, FDI generating reforms, the New Educational Policy, reforms in the defense sector, administrative reforms, and all other transforming reforms by the Modi led government will boost the status of the countries progress and development parameters.

Meeting with the Expectations

All these reforms are placed as fulfilling expectations of the people from their leader and the government. Their hope and desire to be part of a good developed cultural society is sustained by the government under the leadership of Narendra Modi.

Potential to be a Superpower

India has the potential to be a superpower in the near future as a major economy and a powerful defence power in the world.

India's infrastructure projects and economic self-sufficiency will help to achieve the goals.

Infra Projects

The National Infrastructure Pipeline is a set of proposed infrastructure projects for energy, rail projects, highway projects, and urban development projects. Let's go through some major projects.

Sagarmala project is proposed to create waterways and ports across all major places along the coastline of India. It consists of the development of fourteen major coastal economic zones to boost economic activities along the ports.

Bharatmala project consists of the diamond quadrilateral, the golden quadrilateral, national highway development project, north-south, and east-west corridor.

There are ongoing constructions of the expressway at major highways and Setu Bharatam project which is considered of building flyovers on all national highways at all railway crossings across India.

The Diamond Quadrilateral is a project of developing a high-speed network among the four metro cities across India and works of creating dedicated freight corridors and modern rail stations are underway.

Economic Self-Sufficient

Atmanirbhar Bharat is an initiative of the Modi Government to promote Micro, Small & Medium Enterprises (MSMEs) by providing economic assistance and encouragements. Its objective is to encourage creating an influence of the indigenous products and businesses at the international level and making them more competent.

Thus it is clear that definitely India will lead the world in the coming future in terms of economy, as a global power player, epicenter of spirituality, and cultural heritage. And will be a leading superpower as 'Vishwaguru'.

1.5 MAJOR IT PLAYERS

TOPIC BASED CONCEPTS

Evolutions in Information Technology and Computer Science brought mind-blowing changes in the quality of life of the people and developments in the world. United States has produced most of the IT giants in the world. India shares an important role in the IT sector in the world and India is also a major software hub for the world.

IT Sector in the United States

<u>Leading IT Brands</u>

Silicon Valley has become a prominent and largest area of producing IT giants and start-ups in the United States.

Amazon, Google, Microsoft, Apple, and Facebook are considered the big five technology companies having headquarters in the US. Along with these, there are many US-based tech giants that are leading the World's IT Industry.

India as an IT Hub

<u>World-Class IT Infrastructures</u>

India has developed Special Economic Zones and infrastructures providing all the required facilities for software firms, tech hubs, innovation centers, and incubators to start-ups. India plays an important role in the global IT sector with a major share of contribution to the world class innovations.

Software Development, App Development, Cloud Computing, Financial Technology, Information Architecture, Internet of Things (IoT), Artificial Intelligence (AI), and Research & Development in Advance Computing in such every fields India is leading the world. India generates most of the IT brains, talents, executives, and high-profile CEOs throughout the globe. India is also a huge market for online web-based industries and brands.

2. Top Rated

2.1 SKYSCAPERS IN THE WORLD

Overview

We are sometimes very excited to know about the skyscrapers in our city. Let's have a quick overview of some tallest and proposed skyscrapers around the world.

Tallest Skyscrapers

Burj Khalifa in Dubai, UAE is the tallest building in the world having 163 floors and 828 meters in height. One World Trade Center building is the tallest one in the United States situated in New York City with 104 floors and 541.3 meters in height. Shanghai Tower in China and Lotte World Tower in South Korea are among the other tallest skyscrapers in the world. Lodha The Park 1 is the tallest building in India. At present, there are near about a hundred skyscrapers in the world having height more than 300 meters.

Proposed Skyscrapers

Jeddah Tower in Saudi Arabia with a planned height of 1000 meters will be the world's tallest very soon. There are near about 30 to 40 towers of heights above 300 meters are proposed and under construction throughout the world.

2.2 TALLEST STATUES IN THE WORLD

36

It is very interesting to know about the tallest statues in the world. Let's have a quick overview of some tallest statues around the world.

Statue of Unity is the tallest Statue in the world. The statue is of Sardar Vallabhbhai Patel known as the 'Iron Man' of India and was the first deputy prime minister and first home minister of India. It is situated at Sardar Sarovar Dam in the state of Gujrat, India. Its height is 182 meter that is the highest in the world.

The Statue of Liberty situated in New York City of United States, Christ the Redeemer in Rio de Janeiro City of Brazil, Spring Temple Buddha statue in china, Peter the Great Statue in Russia, are among the other well known tallest statues in the world.

Statue of Ram is the proposed tallest statue in the world to be constructed on the bank of river 'Sharayu' in Ayodhya, Uttar Pradesh, India. Also, The Chhatrapati Shivaji Maharaj Smarak is one of the tallest monuments under construction and to be located in the sea near the coastal area of Mumbai City, India.

2.3 NOTEWORTHY WEB PORTALS

Here is the list of some top noteworthy websites for the categories of interests and type of information you need to know.

Nobleprize.org

This website gives you information about all Noble prize winners from 1901 to the present. Here you can find how many Noble laureates are there from your country and around the world. There you can find a list of Nobel Prize winners of each year in all categories.

Oscars.org

This website shows information about all Academy Awards winners of each year in all categories with the list of nominations.

Forbes.com

Here you can find the list of billionaires of the world. It also shows a country-wise list of billionaires. It shows a list of top-ranking companies with their assets.

2.4 COLLEGES AND UNIVERSITIES WORLDWIDE

Education in India

India has an enormous well-established educational structure of study materials and learning institutions. New Educational Policy proposed by the Indian Government will transform India into an educational epicenter of the world.

Colleges and universities in India are demonstrating a great role on the world stage. Indian Institute of Technology (IITs), Indian Institute of Management (IIMs), All India Institute Of Medical Science (AIIMS), Film and Television Institute of India (FTII), National Defence Academy (NDA), Armed Forces Medical College (AFMC), College of Military Engineering (COME) are the prestigious Institutions in India creating a pool of talents who leads various sectors around the globe with their superior brain capacity.

There are more than 700 universities and more than 40,000 colleges in India. They have a good educational infrastructure with advanced facilities like laboratories and libraries.

Science and Technology, Arts and Culture, Business and Laws, Sports & Medicines, Ayurveda and Yoga, Spirituality and Religious Studies, in almost all field of education, India has a great contribution to the world in terms of knowledge, expertise, and values

Education around the World

USA, Australia, Europe, and India are the desired destinations of students and researchers around the world for taking good and quality higher education.

Massachusetts Institute of Technology, Stanford University, and Harvard University are the world's top-ranking universities present in the United States of America. Princeton University, Harvard University, Columbia University, Yale University, Cornell University, Brown University, Dartmouth College, and the University of Pennsylvania, are some of The Ivy League members universities in the United States having world-class recognition and reputation.

Imperial College London, University of Cambridge, University College London, and Swiss Federal Institute of Technology in Zurich are the leading institutions in Europe. The University of Sydney and The University of Melbourne in Australia, Saint Petersburg State University and Lomonosov Moscow State University in Russia are among the other prominent universities in the world.

2.5 LANGUAGES OF THE WORLD

The basic parent families of languages are Indo-European languages, Dravidian language family, and Sino Tibetan languages. There are more than 7000 languages are spoken in the world.

Widely spoken languages in the world are Mandarin Chinese, Spanish, English, Hindi, French, German, Japanese, Russian, Urdu, Arabic, etc. There are 1.2 billion total no. of speakers of the English language; 1.1 billion speakers of Mandarin Chinese, and 600 million speakers of the Hindi language. The modern English language is being spoken all over the world and considered to be one of the commonly used international languages.

India has 122 major languages and more than 1500 spoken languages. Some major Indic languages are Hindi, Bengali, Marathi, Telugu, Tamil, Gujrati, Punjabi, and Sanskrit. Sanskrit is one of the oldest languages in the world and most ancient epics and scriptures are found written in Sanskrit Language. Sanskrit is being studied not in India but also in prominent universities in the world.

3. The Way of Life

TOPIC BASED CONCEPTS

3.1 MAGNIFICENCE IN HINDUISM

TOPIC BASED CONCEPTS

Sanātana Dharma

Religion always teaches us to follow ethics for the sake of humanity. We must identify our roots and follow the good traditional values and teaching of our ancestors and elders in the home. Being modern doesn't mean not to identify and follow them. We must follow a set of rules by our religion and culture

Hinduism referred to 'Sanātana Dharma' is the most ancient and oldest religion in the world and the way of a beautiful life. Every tradition and festivals in Hindu culture are having scientific bases; most of them are being proved right with respect to circumstances and time. Hinduism has evolutionary and persistent thoughts of culture.

Teachings of Hinduism are very prolific and can be learned from different Hindu Scriptures. Those are Vedas, Upanishads, Puranas, Ramayana, Mahabharata, Srimad Bhagavad Gita, Srimad Bhagavatam, etc.

Ayurveda and Yoga are the most precious practices that evolved in Hindu traditions. You will find a dynamic change in your life if you practice these in your life.

India is a land of 'Yogis' from ancient times and enriched with all the resources of spirituality and ways of living life in a beautiful and powerful manner.

Deities in Hinduism

Let's try to understand some divine powers in Hinduism in a few words.

Lord 'Shri Ganesh' and 'Shri Hanuman' have the virtues that to be possessed by youth. They represent the form of purity of thoughts, physical and mental strength, and energy of life.

The Power of Rama's spirit and Krishna's existence is the utmost power for an individual in 'Sthiti' mode and power maintaining universal creation. Be in Krishna Consciousness all the time. 'Rama' is always in the chant by 'Shiv Tattva' and God 'Shiva' is worshiped by a 'Vishnu Tattva'. The chanting of 'Rama' fulfills all aspects of thoughts in the aspirants and it gives 'Chir Santushti' (Eternal Satisfaction) to everything within all.

Goddesses 'Saraswati', 'Lakshmi', and 'Parvati' always care for us like this mother earth, 'Adishakti', The Primal Energy will never leave you alone in this universe and provide you with everything you really deserved and wished for by God, at the right time.

'Shri Datta Shakti' is an intensive power to eradicate and throw away negative ill power in the infected person and the surrounding. Understanding 'Datta Shakti' could prove a powerful technique to realize 'Shuddha Tej' (Pure Spirit Brilliance) and 'Bhav' (Emotion).

The 'Navnath' tradition and the way of life prescribed and practiced by 'Navnathas' are really of exceptional qualities and are truly beautiful.

'Kalki', the incarnation of God 'Vishnu' is believed to appear in 'Kali Yuga' to normalize the mindset of the human being and empower them with eternal spiritual knowledge. There should be a movement to start the awakening of the Lord 'Kalki'.

Adi Shankara, Tulsidas, Chaitanya Mahaprabhu, Narasimha Saraswati, Meerabai, Sant Dnyaneshwar, Eknath Maharaj, Namdeo Maharaj, Sant Tukaram, Samarth Ramdas, Swami Samarth Maharaj, Gajanan Maharaj, Sai Baba, Sri Ramkrishna Paramahamsa, Swami Vivekananda, A.C. Bhaktivedanta Swami Prabhupada these are some prominent saints in Hinduism.

3.2 TEMPLES IN INDIA

Idolatry and Temples

Temples and all other sanctums are the epicenters of divine energy. These sanctums are the 'Shakti Pithas' and idols of Gods and Goddesses in the temples act as sources of energy that spreads positivity and protects us from all kinds of negativity.

There is a certain cause of the existence of sanctums throughout the world. These are the sacred directional headquarters of mankind and global activities.

Let's have an overview of temples having special importance in Hinduism.

Ganesh Temples

Ashtavinayak temples in Maharashtra have significance in the worship of Lord Ganesha. Those are Mayureshwar (Morgaon), Siddhivinayak (Siddhatek), Ballaleshwar (Pali), Varadavinayak (Mahad), Chintamani (Theur), Girijatmaj (Lenyadri), Vighneshwar (Ozar), Mahaganapati (Ranjangaon). Apart from these Siddhivinayak Temple of Mumbai, Dagdusheth Ganpati of Pune, Ganesh Temple at Ganpatipule

Twelve Jyotirlinga

Somnath in Gujarat, Mallikarjuna in Srisailam, Mahakaleswar in Ujjain, Mamleshwar in Omkareshwaram, Kedarnath in Rudraprayag, Bhimashankar in Dakinya, Vishwanath in Varanasi, Trimbakeshwar in Nashik, Baidyanath in Deoghar, Nageshwara in Dwarka, Ramanathaswamy in Rameshwaram, and Grishneshwar in Aurangabad these are the twelve Jyotirlinga.

Shakti Peethas

There are 52 or 108 Shakti Peethas according to various references.

Vaishnodevi Temple, Mahalakshmi Temple of Ambabai at Kolhapur, Tulja Bhawani Temple of Tuljapur, Saptashrungi Temple of Vani, Renuka Devi Temple of Mahur, Amba Devi Temple of Amravati, Dakshineshwari Temple of Mahakali, Mahakali Temple of Ujjain, Vishalakshi Temple of Varanasi, Sharda Devi Temple of Kashmir, Gayatri Temple at Pushkar, these are some of the prominent Shakti Peethas.

Char Dham

'Char Dham' refers to the four abodes devoted to Lord Vishnu. Those are Puri, Rameswaram, Dwarka, and Badrinath.

Other Prominent Temples

Ayodhya, Mathura Vrindavan, Vitthal Mandir Pandharpur, Tirupathi Balaji, Shri Datta Kshetra Gangapur, Shani Shingnapur, Baba Amarnath, ISKCON Temples, and Swaminarayan Temples are some more prominent temples in India.

3.3 KNOW ABOUT HINDU FESTIVALS

Colors of Joy

Hinduism is the most ancient and oldest religion in the world and the way of a beautiful life. Every tradition and festivals in Hindu culture are having scientific bases, most of which are being proved right with respect to circumstances and time. Hinduism has evolutionary and persistent thoughts of culture. Let's have an overview of major festivals celebrated in Hinduism.

Gudipadwa

On the arrival of spring, Gudipadwa is celebrated in India and this festival is considered one of the very auspicious occasions.

Shri Ram Navmi

Celebration of Birth of Prabhu Shri Rama in the Chaitra Navratri set up a pleasant atmosphere in India on Ram Navmi.

Hanuman Jayati

Hanuman Jayanti is celebrated in India on Chaitra Pournimaa. It is the celebration of the birth of Lord Hanuman.

Vat Purnima

Vat Purnima is an important festival for married women in India. A woman prays for the long life and well being of her husband and tie threads around a banyan tree.

Nagpanchami

Nagdevata (Snake) is worshiped on this day in India.

Raksha Bandhan

On this day sisters tie a 'Rakhi' around the wrists of their brothers. It is about the care and affection between brothers and sisters.

Shri Krishna Janmashtami

The birth of Lord Krishna is celebrated on this day with hearts full of joy and happiness. Lord Krishna is an incarnation of Lord Vishnu.

Pola

Pola is the festival celebrated to give respect to the bulls and oxen especially by the farmers in India.

Ganesh Chaturthi

Idols of Lord Ganesh are worshiped during this festival at home and at public Pandals. Ganesha is honored before beginning any task and Ganesha is considered to be the deity of intellect and wisdom.

Navratri

Goddess Durga is worshiped for nine days collectively called as Navratri. It is about the worship of all forms of 'Adishakti', The Primal Energy responsible for the birth of everything in the universe.

Dussehra

The festival of Dussehra is a celebration of the victory of goodness over the ill sentiments.

Dipawali

Dipawali is the festival of lights and the most important festival in Hinduism. It is about celebrating the victory of light, knowledge over the darkness.

Datta Jayanti

The birth of Dattatreya, the incarnation of 'Trimurti' is supposed very spiritual and auspicious celebrations in Hinduism.

Makar Sankranti

Makar Sankranti is celebrated in January month to mark the winter solstice in India

Maha Shivaratri

Maha Shivaratri is celebrated in India by worshiping Lord Shiva. Abundant spiritual energy can be experienced on the night of Maha Shivratri. This festival is a very spiritual veneration.

Holi

Holi is a festival of colors and a festival of spring in India.

3.4 THE SPIRITUAL WORLD

Spiritual Knowledge

Ancient spiritual knowledge in the world can guide the eastern and western waves of thoughts. Spiritual knowledge and structures of its constituents are almost similar throughout all the related concepts in the world. Ancient spiritual knowledge present anywhere is eternal and cannot be completely destroyed by invaders.

Be in love with reading Holy Scriptures and spiritual books and references. Improve your spiritual knowledge by getting familiar with the concepts within it regularly.

Opt for Spirituality

Bring positivity around you and it starts with very small things. Worship the divine power and its manifestation whatever the idea about it is in your understanding and you are following.

Spirituality is the essence of life; it is the source of all of the divine power. Learning methods and teachings of spirituality is the way to come out of all pain and suffering in the materialistic expectations.

Continue meditation on spirituality and chanting of holy mantras is a very essential factor of life for the human being to keep his mind pure ever. Chanting the holy mantra removes impurities in your mind and makes it more stable and pious.

Keeping the mind busy with positive activities is a continuous process; you have to keep alive the spirit every time and continue with spiritual chanting. Stay firm with your feet rooted on the ground. A person when generally goes with excessive pride discontinues chanting and connection with spirituality.

Sometimes we don't realize, it doesn't mean that the activities and changes around you are not taking place. Keep the flag of the divine spirit always flying in your divine circle? It will eradicate all evil spirits within its sphere. Positive vibes attract more positive spirit and prosperity, so always busy doing more and more positive activities.

Spiritual Circle

A change in you with worship and awaking is in one's fate and can be easily received through sensations of positivity in the surrounding. Identify them and get involved. The spiritual circle of God does exist among the creations of the universe. We are the descendants of the spiritual circle; we are part of it and so we have to behave with some responsibilities and discipline. Say this while standing and praying in front of God. Our journey starts with it. Marching towards a good vision is helpful for oneself and the rest of the world too. To dissolve in the positive and eternal spiritual circle is real eternal happiness.

Spiritual Maturity

The maturity level of the world is constantly changing and attaining success depends on it. The maturity level is an important factor in the journey of life to success. Spiritual maturity makes you become more powerful with perceptible knowledge. The human mind is always tending to learn anything if provided in simplified methods. One can easily create interest in spirituality if the material is provided with the simplification 'Sahaj', and it is really available in that form indeed.

The Spirituality

The method of 'Pap Kshalan' (Sin Elimination) is to light up with chanting divine 'Mantra' and living the life honestly with truthfulness. Then consider fruits of your wrongdoing are minimized to a minimum level, which means you will have to suffer for a little rather than worst. Link yourself up with positivity to find opportunities around you.

Have some fifteen minutes of 'Nitya Vandana' (Daily Prayer) and chanting in spare time throughout the day. Chanting God's divine mantra is the best solution to attain the supreme self in the 'Kali Yuga'. Stay 'Dhyanast' (Meditated) towards the divine which is eternal, all other states in life come and go, even the soul changes the bodies.

'Dhyan' (Meditation), 'Jap' (Chanting), and 'Bhakti Marga' (Path of Devotion) these are the solutions to stay away from the repetition of cycles of life, death, and rebirth. Clean up your soul and body like the pure sacrifices in holy 'Yagya'. Always chant in mind devotional songs or mantras.

'Shuddha Bhav' sacredness is the soul of your body like the sun rays. One can say got 'Mokshya' (Eternal Enlightenment), maybe that when his soul got merged with sun rays. Like sun rays the time and millennium have their virtues depends on power after its reach. The first sunray has the power to create 'Muhūrt' (An auspicious moment). Knowledge grows like the power of sun rays. A single source of energy can light up everything and has the power to create waves of spirituality.

Do all Rituals and 'Sanskara' (Rites) on your soul, repair your soul. This should be your main task each day. Shift your focus on 'Mastishka' (The Brain). Always stay connected with the divine spirit and make it your daily habit.

All in different 'Sampradaya' communities are one if considered everyone as soul. The level of knowledge is maintained by the soul and it happens to have partial and multiple rebirths depending on the wishlist and its nature, within its sphere. The concept of 'Vishwarup Darshan' should be understood with clarity, in accordance with diversities in the world.

'Vairagya' (Asceticism) and 'Prabodhanam' (Awakening) should be the main aspect of the life of some. So awake and get united to raise spiritual maturity among people. The unified efforts of all of us can bring applicable results.

TOPIC BASED CONCEPTS

3.5 THE ISKCON MOVEMENT

About ISKCON

ISKCON is one of the leading movements of the time and revives the principles of the divine spirit of Lord Krishna.

The International Society for Krishna Consciousness (ISKCON) was established in 1966 in New York City by A. C. Bhaktivedanta Swami Prabhupada. He was an Indian spiritual teacher, influential 'Vaishnava' monk and a religious scholar in Hinduism. Based on the principles of 'Bhakti Yoga' ISKCON is spreading colors of joy in spirituality and humanity by its services offered all over the world through the strong network of full-time practitioners, devotees, followers, temples, and publications.

Krishna is the eighth 'Avatar' incarnation of God Vishnu and considered to be the supreme personality of God in 'Vaishnavism'. One can greatly understand Krishna Consciousness by understanding the verses of Śrīmad Bhagavad Gītā.

Presence

ISKCON has its presence all over the world in almost all countries having near about 850 temples build up in the service of Lord Krishna along with wide publications of books on Krishna Consciousness and spirituality. The ISKCON movement is now part of the life of the millions of followers around the world whether in North America or South America, Europe, Africa, Asia, and almost in all countries over the continents.

The Devotees

One should follow few things in life to become a true devotee at ISKCON, let's understand those. At first, become a vegetarian and take only offered blessed food, second most important is to start reading and understanding Śrīmad Bhagavad Gītā and Śrīmad Bhāgavatam. Start knowing about ISKCON culture by connecting with its center and temple in your area.

The mission of one's life should be to empower oneself and humans, spending this life in the service of God, and keep chanting his holy Mahamantra:

Hare Kṛṣṇa Hare Kṛṣṇa

Kṛṣṇa Kṛṣṇa Hare Hare

Hare Rāma Hare Rāma

Rāma Rāma Hare Hare

3.6 WE SHOULD CARE

TOPIC BASED CONCEPTS

Transform

Unless the basic thought and principles of living standards of the people do not change and purified with spirituality, there will no eradication of pain, suffering, depression, poverty, disputes, and corruption in society. Each one of us has to start the initiative with ourselves. Live the life with principles along with purifications of thoughts and actions. You will always find the help and solutions to your problems around you within your reach, only the thing is that you have to identify and grasp them. This life is an opportunity to get out of the process of birth and death cycles. Good actions 'Karma' is the only solution to all.

Review Inside

Nothing is more important than taking care of your parents. What they have done for you is always uncountable. Your first duty is to make a deep obeisance towards your parents and take care of them for the rest of your life.

We Must Act Now

There is a vast portion of the population in the world is under the poverty level and living not even with safety standards. Take care of needy people as much you can if you have the capacity within you and pull them towards enlightenment, thus you can best return to 'Samajrun'. It doesn't take much, to spread knowledge and awareness in the society about living a good life full of discipline and good values within the culture.

Life with reduced necessities can set a very good example for others, following and looking towards you. Open up your mind to the spiritual nature of the world and allow your mind to flow through it. Reducing the accumulation of necessities can save more in your life and that will generate a surplus which can help to reduce poverty to some extent.

Wide Spectrum

There should be places of worship at every mile. These sanctums should have good infrastructure. Daily availability of 'Mahaprasadam' (Blessed Food) for the poor and needy people within its sphere must be facilitated by the temple trusts. Also, the basic needs of them should be taken care of. There should be centers delivering spiritual knowledge and doing active charity works, nearby all the holy places.

There should be love and care for animals as like to honor companion living beings. We should respect their existence and importance in nature. Try to be vegetarian and try to avoid the intake of the non-vegetarian meals. We should not feed our stomachs by killing innocent animals. Such non-vegetarian food may produce impure thoughts and bad habits in your nature.

Cleanliness must be maintained at all public places. The habit of cleanliness is being developed in schools nowadays, but somewhere some of the elders do not have habits of keeping cleanliness. Educating about social etiquettes and encouraging personal responsibility about maintaining hygiene and cleanliness will really work.

Eco-friendly concepts should be implemented within all types of development projects. Enough plantations of different fruit-bearing trees should be there all over possible places. We must encourage forestation around the globe to cover up the earth with greenery.

Water pollution is a major concern throughout the world. We must have some measures to ensure clean water flow in rivers and lakes. The contamination of water in the rivers must be avoided. Reservoirs of potable water should be increased all over the deprived locations; otherwise, there would be severe consequences in the future.

How good is the human being if the humans themselves are not taking care of his Mother Earth? We must bow to our only one Mother Earth. Become nature friendly and adopt a life culture preserving the environment.

4. Analysis

4.1 PHILOSOPHY
AN APPROACH

Philosophy is the study of basic questions and perceptions about thoughts, values, knowledge, ethics, and mental states. It can be categorized as Western Philosophy and Eastern Philosophy. Indian Philosophy mainly consists of Hindu Philosophy, Jain philosophy, and Buddhist philosophy.

Schools of Hindu Philosophy are classified as Nyaya, Vaisheshika, Samkhya, Yoga, Mimansa, and Vedanta. Adi Shankara is one of the most revered Hindu philosophers. Kapila, Patañjali, Yajnavalkya, Vyasa, Gautama, Vātsyāyana, Kanada, Jaimini, Gaudapada, Yamunacharya, Madhvacharya, Chaitanya Mahaprabhu, and Goswamis of Vrindavan are the notable philosophers in Hinduism.

Ashtanga Yoga given in the Yoga Sutras of Patanjali are Yamas, Niyama, Asana, Pranayama, Pratyahara, Dharana, Dhyana, and Samadhi.

One of the most powerful sources of philosophical knowledge in the world is Śrīmad Bhagavad Gītā. It provides the human being with the concepts of thoughts and directive principles. It fills us with real authentic spiritual and philosophical knowledge. Śrīmad Bhagavad Gītā explains about Jnana Yoga, Bhakti Yoga, Karma Yoga, and Raja Yoga.

4.2 HISTORY OF THE LIFE ON THIS PLANET

96

Evolution of Life

Evolutionary biology explains how life started on the earth with the evolution of fossil organisms according to fossil evidences. Furthermore among the many theories proposed about the evolution of life on this planet, the notable one theory is Darwin's evolutionary theory.

Ancient Civilizations

Indus Valley Civilization dated approximately 4,000 years ago is considered as the most advanced ancient civilization in the history of the world according to the findings by archeological surveys.

Vedic Period

In the history of India Vedic culture has great importance. Creations of Vedic texts like Vedas, Upanishads, and The Grammar of Panini were significant in the history of mankind.

Religious Millennium

The first millennium was the period of religious evolutions and establishments. There were peaceful coexistences of Hinduism, Buddhism, Islam, and Christianity in the world.

Second Millennium

One may call it the millennium of the evolution of modern culture and society with the establishment of nationalism throughout the world. It can be described as the era of scientific inventions, creation of knowledge resources, classification of literature, astronomical findings and space missions, new age infrastructure, urban revolution, and the digital world.

Third Millennium

This millennium has great hope and expectations about the peaceful existence of human beings and ecological balance. This is the only challenge in relation to contemporary events on this planet.

There will be a transformation in human life due to increasing brain capabilities. Also, we may be accompanied by some extraterrestrial intelligence in this millennium.

4.3 KNOW ABOUT DEFENCE DOCTRINE

Defence Doctrine also called Military Doctrine is a kind of detailed report on strategies and planning of actions related to military operations and defence activities. Experts on military and defence strategies outline detailed plans on defence procurement, armament, military tactics, and countermeasures. It also suggests about missile defence system, space and cyberspace protection plans, nuclear and non-nuclear strategies.

Modern Warfare

Defence doctrine plays an important role in activities involved in modern changing warfare strategies. Information warfare and psychological warfare are considered to be the most strategically important lookout while creating a new-age defence doctrine.

Top Strategist

Army doctrines developed by The United States, India, and Russia are some of the most superior defence documents in the world related to the defence and strategic studies.

India has great expertise in making strategic plans and has intellectual defence doctrines.

4.4 SCHIZOPHRENIA CAN BE CURED

104

Overview

Most of the people in the world are having some symptoms partially similar to schizophrenic symptoms and that they even don't come to know. It is the darkness and fear of negativity. It is widely present everywhere. A person suffering from schizophrenia finds it difficult for him to organize a course of action. The general form of behaviors and process of work should be followed by the person to get out of mental illness as early as possible. Concepts of universality and oneness help to solve problems of misconceptions.

Set up Your State of Mind

Feed up yourself with good habits and strategize a fixed daily routine busy with a full day of simplified activities. Choose your profession suitable to your nature and calculations of mental ability. Supportive study of the art stream along with creativity will be found more helpful to repair your thought process easily in less time with fewer efforts.

Abstract art and its visual study can help out to solve the puzzles of visual distractions. Keep your mind and its activities under observation to understanding its nature and inclinations.

Meditation helps you to pack up the thoughts that are unfolded and scattered with your confrontations with the environment. Remove all unnecessary thoughts within your mind and keep your mind always focused.

A curb of discipline and moral support of others will be found and received at every step in life. You only have to catch that yourself to get out of the situation. Others can help you, but tackling the puzzles of distractions in your mind and organizing the thought process has to be worked out by yourself. Others may provide you moral support and exemptions.

Enhance your capabilities.

Extraordinary acknowledgments are being developed while dealing with schizophrenic symptoms in order to improve and treat well. Take benefits of the developed qualities handling the symptoms like hallucinations and continual thought process in a positive and creative manner. Inject spiritual guidelines into the hallucinations.

Exceed your social interactional communication through proper channels and comprehensive sessions inclusive of spiritual teaching. Elevate your moral values while interacting with social elements. Moral and spiritual teachings build your basic concepts of life.

Intensive reading on different topics and subjects will guide you to overcome delusions. General concepts and facts that come along while reading different books and articles will assist you to form your good sense of perception.

Only the purification of thoughts and behavior will be found more advantageous in the healing process. If the thought process is very clear and simplified, it gives rise to organized speech and actions. So focus on improving your thoughts and ideas at the root level.

Motivate yourself at an accelerated level and redefine your ideas with the help of planning of actions to fulfill your ambitions in life. Ambitions to do something good for you and the rest of the world by motivating and helping others will guide you with the way to subside the negativity in thoughts.

Finally

Medication and meditation on improving the thought process at the base level, both are equally important for the treatment of schizophrenia as it is treatable.

So get ready and prepare for a beautiful sunrise waiting for you ahead with a lot of interesting experiences of emotional nurturing.

5. Curiosity

5.1 ALIENS ARE COMING

Do Aliens Know About Us?

The alien world may have encouraged and encountered the earth many times before, which we don't know. We are not alone in the universe.

In the last century, we have seen a technological boost due to the invention of computers and in this century we may definitely confront aliens from other planets or outer space. That event could be immensely great and good as if life-changing for us and our planet. Else maybe we enslaved by them or maybe a complete disaster.

Question is that do aliens know us. Maybe yes, they may be watching us from long time and life expectancy on other planets maybe more than a thousand year.

UFO Sightings

There is a deep study on Aliens and UFO sightings by armature enthusiasts all over the world. Evidences regarding encounter of aliens or unidentified flying objects (UFOs) are suspected to be present by giving references of the different theories and incidents that occurred in the past and in the history.

Roswell UFO crash, Battle of Los Angeles, Miracle of the Sun, Gorman Dogfight are some of the widely discussed theories about alien encounters and UFO sightings. Among them Roswell UFO Crash is the most popular incident about alien life.

Extraterrestrial Life

The presence of extraterrestrial life in outer place will be definitely confirmed in this century with the help of hi-tech mechanisms of detection and identifications of life. Findings about the existence of Exoplanets and Super-Earths with awaiting more details are on the way to let us know more about Extraterrestrial life. We are going to catch the alien world in the cosmos very soon.

5.2 MYSTERIES OF OUR UNIVERSE

There is an ocean of mysteries in the history of mankind from the evolution. Let's have a quick review of notable topics of mysteries in the universe.

Lost Island of Atlantis

It is said that there was an island in the middle of the Atlantic Ocean named Atlantis. The references of the existence of the island were supposed to be in the stories by Plato. Atlantis might be an ancient developed civilization lost in the ocean.

Underwater City of Dwarka

'Dwarkapuri' of Krishna was founded on the coastal area of Gujrat. And it is being proved by archeologists that the remains and old structures of 'Dwarka' exist underwater at the Gulf of Cambay. Due to sea-level rise caused over a long period of time the city may have lost its luster.

The Bermuda Triangle

The Bermuda Triangle can be identified as a triangular region in the North Atlantic Ocean near the south east of Florida. It is said that planes and ships crossing the region get disappeared in the region due to the magnetic power of the ocean and the result of volcanic eruptions at the bottom. But there is no trusted source of information approving the existence of such a mysterious area.

'Yeti' The Snowman

Often widely discussed fictitious giant creatures believed to exist in the mountain regions covered with snow. Yeti footprints are caught in the cameras many times throughout the world in snow glaciers sectors.

Black Holes

Black Holes are the specific regions of magnetic fields in the universe where the energy particles even disappear and the large size of clusters of stars get absorbed in the darkness. It might be also a result of gravitational collapse in the region. Super massive black holes in the universe take away giant stars and galaxies.

Dark Matter

Dark matter is full of the major portion of the spaced apart from actual matter and is an invisible form of matter which also exists in the universe. It has been always a point of intellectual arguments about the existence of the universe.

The Multiverse

The concept of Multiverse is very popular in space theories. It suggests that the multiple forms of the same universe may exist and may have the same properties and nature. There are also unproved theories about the existence of the parallel universes.

5.3 KNOW THE OUTER SPACE

We are not capable of imagining the edge of the endless universe. We could now get our reach beyond our solar system. Unmanned robotic space missions are still searching the evidences of life on other planets in outer space. There will be a confrontation with extraterrestrial life very soon in the future.

Solar System

Moving around the Sun our solar system has inner planets Mercury, Venus, Earth, Mars, and outer planets Jupiter, Saturn, Uranus, Neptune. And beyond that, there is Kuiper Belt.

Identifying Our location

Our solar system is present in the local interstellar cloud near the inner rim of the Orion Arm of the Milky Way Galaxy. Milky Way Galaxy is part of The Local Galactic Group which is present in the Virgo Super Cluster. Virgo Super Cluster along with its group of Local Super Clusters can be identified in the observable universe.

Other Components

Asteroids, Comets, Dwarf Planet, Super-Earths, Habitat Zones, Exoplanets, Nebulas, Stars,

Constellations, Molecular Clouds, and Galaxies are the different entities constituent the universe.

5.4 MYTHOLOGIES OF THE WORLD

Mythologies around the world are always areas of interest for historians and amateurs in the world. Classical mythologies like Greek mythology and Roman mythology are popularly being studied in the world and influenced most of the enthusiastic people. Let's have an overview of some classical mythologies.

Greek Mythology

Greek mythology is described in stories of the ancient world about deities and characters. Story of the Trojan War and poems like The Lliad, The Odyssey are prime faces of Greek mythology.

Roman Mythology

Roman mythology is full of adventurous stories moving around the deities of the mythological era. The story of The Aeneid and Livy plays an important role in studies of Roman Mythology.

Roman Mythology consists of practices and beliefs related to twelve major deities.

Those are Vulcan (God of Fire), Vesta (Daughter of Saturn and Ops), Apollo (Oracular God) and Diana, Juno (The Wife of Jupiter), Venus (The God of Love) and Mars (The God of War), Mercury and

Ceres (Goddess of Agriculture), Neptune (God of Water) and Minerva (Goddess of Wisdom)

6. Art & Design

6.1 USER INTERFACE DESIGN
AN OVERVIEW

Understanding UID

User interface design is the art of designing interfaces for devices like computers; mobiles and machines while human interaction. The role of the user interface designer is to design the interfaces within the layouts with the help of design elements.

Process of UID

It starts with making the list of the requirements such as what type of functionalities will be there on your screen, deciding the positions of the logo, top navigation, and content appearance. If you are provided with the ready wireframes, then it is good to go ahead.

Before that, we must check the aspects of usability. What kind of users you are going to deal with and what the user will do with the system. How he will navigate throughout the screen.

Then it comes, deciding the color scheme, and making a library of required stock images. For organizing content, you must take account of the hierarchy and the importance of placements of the data at the right place.

Finally, start with the design to give look and fill

using the design elements. This was about the process of UID.

Features of your UID

Your User Interface should be designed in a well-organized structured concept with simplicity. Design components should follow the principles of usability and should be easy to reuse. The design should meet with the user's expectations to drive the user's attention.

There should be consistency maintained designing the interfaces. The content should have clarity and clear visibility. The color schemes should be followed by the brand guideline and the overall look should be very fascinating.

Some of the related concepts you need to know.

Human-Computer Interaction (i.e. HCI),
Heuristic Techniques,
Concept of Usability,
Understanding and creating style guides,
Color theory and Design Elements

6.2 VISUAL DESIGN CONCEPTS

Understanding Visual Design

Visual design involves the process of creating ideas and concepts of graphic design on a digital platform by using design elements, typography, stock images, and content.

Scope of Visual Design

The visual design has tremendous scope dealing with the future technologies and trends like App Development, Web UI, Augmented Reality, Internet of Things (IoT) and Artificial Intelligence (AI)

Terms related to Visual Design

Visual design relates with the field of User Interface Design, Graphic Design, Logo Design, Typography, User-Centered Design, User Experience Design, User Interaction Design, Computer-Aided Design, Animation, and Visual Effects.

6.3 DEFINING HUMAN-COMPUTER INTERACTION

Concept of HCI

Study of Human-Computer Interaction is very important while designing interfaces where the human as a user operates and interacts with computers, machines, and all types of tech devices.

The vast field of Human-Computer Interaction involves processes following principles of user interface design, creating a mental model, user-focused design, study of user's behavior, emotions, and thought process.

6.4 KNOW THE COLOR THEORY

Categories of Color Theory

Color Theory is based on the mixing of colors with different variations on the color wheel. According to it, color theory can be categorized as follows.

<u>1. Primary Color</u>

Red, Green, and Blue are popular primary colors on the color wheel.

<u>2. Secondary Color</u>

Orange, Green, and Purple are categorized as secondary color.

<u>3. Tertiary Color</u>

Tertiary colors are created by combinations of primary and secondary colors.

Warm & Cool Colors

Red, Yellow, Orange and variations of these colors are treated as warm colors, while green, blue, and purple colors with their variations are considered cool colors.

Importance of Color Theory

User interface designer are expected to follow the color schemes proposed by the brand guideline. The use of color theory based on the philosophy of the brand creates a greater impact with the creation of brand identity.

6.5 CLASSIC PAINTINGS OF INDIA

Paintings of Raja Ravi Verma

Raja Ravi Verma was the master of the most superior paintings in the history of India. His unique style of paintings sets a great example for all the forthcoming generations of Artists. One must search for his paintings available online for taking a glance at the great heritage of India.

Raja Ravi Varma was born in the princely state of Travancore. He received appreciations for his deep understanding of aesthetic values and Indian traditions. We must always remember his great legacy.

6.6 THE FILMOGRAPHY
AN OUTLINE

Thought Making

Film making and documentation of the activities and thoughts with visual perceptions of the human being is the subject of core interests and creativity. The nature of displaying ideas and pure visions of thought are accompanied with creativity.

Imaginations displayed through the screens take innovative form of ideas to establish changes in forms of human life. They influence the societies and the cultures.

Sci-Fi movies, biographical films, historical films, and informative documentaries have capacities to influence your thought process.

Let's take an overlook of some destinations of Filmography with the rough outline.

Hollywood and Western Film Industries

Hollywood is the abundant source and production hub of creations of motion pictures and performances. It is a great workplace of artists, musicians, writers having great innovative work. Movies made of the western world in English and different European languages create a great impact on the World Cinema.

Notable films of Hollywood and world cinema must be watched sometimes in your life.

Bollywood and Indian Film Industry

Indian film industry has the world's largest number of film productions in the world. Various regional film industries in India contribute to the legendary of the motion picture. Among those Bollywood has a major share in Indian Cinema. Dadasaheb Phalke was a legend in Indian Cinema. He directed and produced the first Indian Movie 'Raja Harishchandra' in 1913.

Award and Recognitions

The prominent motion picture and television awards are The Academy Awards given by the Academy of Motion Picture Arts and Sciences, The Golden Globe Awards, BAFTA Awards by The British Academy of Film and Television Arts, AMY Awards by Australian Interactive Media Industry Association.

The Prominent Awards in India are the Dadasaheb Phalke Award and National Film

Awards by the Directorate of Film Festivals.

Various International Film Festivals around the world are the platforms for the films to get recognitions.

ABOUT THE AUTHOR

Mangesh Dambhare is a writer from Yavatmal, Maharashtra, India. He is a graduate of the University of Pune. He is having more than twelve years of expertise in User Interface and User Experience Design. He is a successful Published Author having a Positive, Constructive, and Optimistic Outlook with exposure to the various Media Platforms. The mission of his life is to Empower Humans through his Books and Initiatives.